hands-on
books

Pleasure-in-relating

Susan Groves

for Ann
(older sister)

First published by Hands-On Books 2013
PO Box 385, Athlone, 7760, Cape Town, South Africa

Copyright © Susan Groves 2013

Editor: Na'eemah Masoet
Cover artwork: 'The Colours of My Daughter' by
Jacobus November (*Big Issue* vendor Spar Milnerton)
Author photograph: Elizabeth Wood
Book and Cover Design by Monique Cleghorn

Set in 10.5 pt on 15 pt Legacy Serif

Printed and bound by Mega Digital, Cape Town

ISBN: 978-1-920590-45-1

Contact Susan Groves at www.susangroves.com

contents

living

loving

EMPTINESS

Form is emptiness.
Emptiness is form.

The Heart Sutra
The Buddha[1]

1. Siddhartha Gautama.

emptiness

spaciousness

I

know

there needs
to be a lot of space

       around
       the words,

       the entries.

The space is
as important
as the
words.

form

Seeking …

(for) a form.

shape of a life

My life too seeks its form.

                              work

    play

                                    silence

        friendship

Swaying together like kelp.

form

family

society

living

loving

trapezes

Dad
would scrape the gates
regularly,
and varnish them.
He made swings and trapezes for us too,
at each of our (three) houses.

And I can hardly knock a nail in.

But, now in my 50s, I find myself wondering about having a swing
in the front garden.

scary

Dad
sat in bed –
like a zombie.
Scary.

Ann told me, years later, they just
closed him
up again.
I thought
they'd operated.

Ma didn't explain.

My father had a brain tumour. I was thirteen. He was discharged
from hospital into the care of Ma, a nurse.

I remember looking through a crack in the door. He lay in
their bed, head shaven after brain surgery. I never went in.
(Peter, my brother, said *he* did.)

I can picture the bed. It had a wooden headboard with green
stripes in the middle. Probably I was conceived in it.

I'm glad he came home. I'm glad you bought him home, Ma.

Aunt Lou came to help nurse him. She said he opened his
eyes whenever Ma came into the room. That made me know
he loved her.

dad's death

I can
experience
kindness as
condescension.

I'm sorry about that.

My dad died on the last day of Standard 5. That helped. It meant
I didn't have to go to school the next day and face sympathy.

Jacqui and I met the beginning of the next term (in high school) as
we travelled on the train together from the same suburb. She tells
me now that I wouldn't talk about his death – that I made it clear
that this topic just wasn't on.

It's taken me a long time to grieve and to wish he hadn't died then.
Thirteen is really quite small.

I'm not ashamed anymore.

the blue dress

I wore
that sort of shiny blue dress
to
Dad's funeral.

I'd used it
for doing the church readings
before.

Hate
stiff dresses.

I remember Gran saying 'Do you know what day it is?' when we
were fooling around on the day of the funeral.

prison

My brother
went to prison.

Kind of blew the
idea that we were
a 'good family'.

Peter – two years younger than me – was ten when our dad died.
I remember him crying inconsolably.

When his youngest child was ten, he was sentenced to three
years in prison for fraud. I pointed out to him, after his release,
that at the time of his being taken away from his family, his
children were the same ages *we* had been when *our* dad was
taken – ten, thirteen, fifteen (and our younger sister, four).

He shrugged indifferently, perhaps with a slight hint of interest.

hands

His
hands.

I know those
hands, but I
don't know how
I know them.

(They are very long, thin and expressive. He used them when
he spoke.)

He had lost a lot of weight in prison – or possibly even after his arrest
– and looked so very different. He had been captured and was forced
into vulnerability. It was the first time I could reach him in a long
long time. I loved the visits, though we were all unsure of ourselves
(each time I went with a friend or sibling).

I would love to have him back, as he was then. My young brother,
with no pretence of bravado, strength or capacity.

When I saw him a few months after his release, this part of him had
flown. And he was large and impenetrable to me again.

I have photos of him as a small boy. One at prayer, one sweeping
with a grass broom. In a soft light.

I'd like to see you in a soft light.

the black box

Does
every family have
a box?

It was always there, at the bottom of Mom's cupboard – the one that fitted right into the wall like a cave. The shiny black box about the size of three shoeboxes – rectangular. I never thought to ask about it. I don't know what I imagined was in there – jewellery maybe?

When Peter went to prison, the children cleared out his flat – a lousy job. Jilly, then ten, came upon the box. She seemed to sense its significance – she was proud of finding it. There was concern over whether its contents were damp. How did I get word of it? When I did, it was as if a huge chunk of history slammed into me. Of course! The box!

And so, slowly, we looked. (Though not until he was out of tjoekie[2].) We found documents detailing the life – and shocking death – of our paternal granddad Albert at sea in the battle of Jutland[3] when Dad was ten. Papers telling of our dad, Fred's, first wife – giving information that allowed us to trace our half-siblings living in South Africa and England. Records of a life we hadn't known too well, with his early death - or it seemed early to us, his second family.

I could get cross that Peter took the box. I wasn't there the day he came to take what he wanted after Mom's death.

2. South African slang for prison.
3. World War 1.

But that isn't really the point. The point is, we found it. And so found more of *him*.

And this goes on.

family

society

living

loving

dreamers

Nontombi dreamed.

Elizabeth dreamed.

Nontombi tells her aunts and her sister of the dream and they plan a ritual – *ibhekile* in isiXhosa. About twenty days later a fire is lit in the yard and the lengthy process of brewing begins.

Day 1: Nontombi eats the porridge (*isidudu somqombothi*) from the traditional brew before it ferments and sends Princess a beautiful picture on her phone of the large black pot on the outside fire.

As the drink ferments over the next few days, various family members stir the brew and commune with their ancestors.

Day 5: Nontombi strains the now well-fermented drink and speaks to her departed relatives, asking their blessing.

Day 6: Nontombi rises at 5.30 on Saturday morning 10 November. She, her sister, brother and paternal aunt go to the graveyard to visit the graves of her mom, dad and paternal grandmother. (These are far apart, she tells me.) The small group explain to their relatives that there'd be a ritual that afternoon.

As neighbours and friends arrive at the home, to each it is explained: 'Nontombi dreamt of her parents and her paternal grandmother. That is why we gather, to acknowledge and remember them'.

It goes on till well after dark. Sharing the *umqombothi* seals this acknowledgement of Nontombi and her ancestors.

I speak to Nontombi the following morning. She says she is exhausted. 'You'll feel different,' I say. 'I feel different already,' she says. 'I feel at peace.'

Elizabeth dreams of her mother. It feels painful. Another person enters the dream and her mother softens.

Elizabeth tells one or two others of the dream. She tells me. I write a poem about it which I send her some time later. Perhaps Elizabeth tells her therapist? I think so.

Does Elizabeth feel at peace? I think something changed.[4]

4. Nontombi's parents have both died tragically in various ways. She is black African and 21. Elizabeth is English and in her 50s. Her dad is still alive at 90.

a gentle tongue

He
has cancer of the tongue.

I think of
all his years
spouting homophobia
from a wealthy (English)
pulpit.

I can't
find
compassion

(but my heart is sore).

shyness

It's
like
with each
encounter
in this
country
with
someone
from
a different
race
there's
a little
bump
to get over
every time.

I don't mind these bumps.

Each person I meet, I meet my pre-judice first. I've almost got to
enjoy it.

I long for us to be curious, interested in this … and to go towards it.

It's not evil.

It's maybe partly shyness?

knickers

'You
lent me your
knickers.
And you bathed in
my water and I
in yours.
I felt excited
because us blacks
had been told
we were dirty'.

Nozipho and I both worked at the hospital – me as social worker, she as cleaner. She needed to flee an abusive husband and so came to stay with me for a while. And, she remembers, I lent her my knickers.

suffering

'In my practice I see people who have suffered greatly – and they
are not black.'

'No, that can't be', he says.

He had lost an eye when, in his dusty township, police fired birdshot
into a protest march of dancing youth. (This in the late 80s.)
We met when he was being fitted with a false eye in the hospital
where I worked. I remember his mother watching over him in
the corner bed as I approached shyly.

Years later, after a short visit, Mzukisi and I are talking as we walk to
book his bus back home.

He grew up in harsh poverty as a black South African.

'Once you've known extreme poverty, you never never want to go
back there', he says.

Everyone's suffering is valid.

unveiled

She
threw back her black
veil and smiled.

It was a
startling moment.

Staying briefly in Birmingham, puzzled by fully veiled women, and noticing my attitude hardening.

Managed to find Katherine Bullock's *Rethinking Muslim Women and the Veil* in the local library[5]. It helped.

Then Mila comes for tea. She's in the full outfit – I forget the name. All in black and her face covered. She comes from the street into the shared passage and enters our living room. On entering here, she flings her face-veil back over her head. She is transformed. She's alive, she's beautiful – she exists. I ask her the questions the book hadn't answered for me.

> Did your husband see you before you were married?
> Have your husband's friends seen you?

The answers: yes to the former, no to the latter. ('We socialise separately'.)

It changed everything.

5.   London: The International Institute of Islamic Thought. 2007 (2nd edition).

family

society

living

loving

snails

Elizabeth W. is teaching me to garden.

'What are
snails good for?'
I ask.
'There must be *something*?'

'Not for anything,'
she says.

Then, after a pause, she adds: 'They're good for birds to eat.'

I take the rusted tin – still smelling of chai tea – to the field.
Please let them still be alive.

I collect snails and transport them – by foot, it's not far – to the field at the end of the road. Sometimes I leave them in the tin for a while – too long. I'm worried I've done it this time.

No, there they are, clinging to the inside of the plastic lid.
Good snails.

I mean, who would live in a world without snails?

CA lung[6]

'There's
been something
happening here.'

(We're on the phone.)

'Yes?' I'm expectant. I'm always somehow waiting for
his life to take off. He's a talented man.

'I've been diagnosed with cancer of the lung.'

He's about 40. Living a good life. Been supportive of me.

First time someone I know shares with me like this.

He's matter-of-fact.

For me it's dramatic.

Only the next day I realise: yes, cancer's a *drama* subject.
I don't want to do it that way.

This feels much better.

6. This is how it would appear in his medical records.

permission for quietness

I've become
good at being noisy,
and
I'm really glad.

And
I often want –
also with others –
to be quiet.

I have only done this a few times. I remember playing guitar
and singing to Veronica. It had to be extremely soft as she was
so sensitive (she suffered from Chronic Fatigue Syndrome).
There was a delicacy in this that was extremely beautiful –
exquisite.

Two people who live in a busy city said to me recently: 'I want
to live more quietly'. In an extrovert culture this is going against
the grain.

It's hard to let new ways of being emerge in ourselves.

pushing

I often feel,
even in just walking,
that I
am *pushing*
myself.

It's subtle but once I spotted it I noticed it everywhere. It's in
the body. Not restful. 'T'll probably take a life-time to unlearn.

things

I like
to take care of
things.

And now and again to make something with my hands. Like at
the guide-scout camp when I was maybe fourteen (after Dad died?).
I made a little stool with a keyhole feature in the side. I loved that
little stool. It went astray with the various moves / tenants.

The word 'material' has at its root *mater* – mother, source.

soft

It is the opening ceremony at Vukani, the tiny meditation
centre we started at Hogsback, Eastern Cape, South Africa.

I place my wishes
by the african genderless
unfired Buddha
that Anton made.
I wrote: a soft place.

That was ten years ago now.
I've found some softness.

And I'm starting
to see
it was my *body*
seeking this.

scribbles from a writing course

How will I know the course has succeeded?

- I've made a new friend/colleague
- I *am* writing/crafting
- I have the means to write – an (electronic) notebook

How will I know if my *life* has succeeded?

it matters

I'm
becoming clear

it's not what I
do
but where I live

from
that matters.

in praise of movement

'A sedentary lifestyle is not ideal for children'. I saw this in a respectable newspaper recently.

The only lines I remember from Obama's biography – the first of them – were something like this – on his visit to a poor inner city pre-school: 'The children were running and jumping, delighting in their mobility'.

On a radio programme on learning challenges, the woman says: 'Movement moulds the structure of the brain. Down, under, beneath ... these are important words for the little one'.

Maybe all our brains need some re-moulding.

abilities

I felt
very alive
when I came from
there.

The classes with Remix felt like a revelation. (They're an integrated
dance company – people with all sorts of 'disabilities' – and
abilities of course.) Nadine, leading us expertly from a wheelchair
with her two legs sort of short and dangly. Zama, double amputee
in a wheelchair – and apparently good at headstands. Andile,
profoundly deaf. Mpotseng – sign-language interpreter. And me,
at the open class. We made a lot of physical contact with each
other, once Zama surprising me – as I crawled on the floor –
by coming up underneath my body and lifting me.

I figured each must have journeyed to a deep appreciation
of their bodies, which is maybe why I felt so free there.

simple words?

'I've decided I can like my life'.

This from a woman who struggles in her life following an upbringing of coldness and dislike.

'I've decided I can like my life'.

Her words stay with me as a koan, a mantra, a guide?

nhs prescription

At an informal evening of music and singing a woman says
she attends *Sing for Life* – a group where some of those
attending are referred by their doctors.

In the National Health Service in England knitting is
prescribed as well as taking time in green spaces.

If it takes a doctor's prescription to get us singing, why not?

legs

Her legs are brown
mine white / beige as we
roll them up to avoid the foam.

I like hers.

Two Susans go for a walk. 'I had a serious accident in 2010,' she says.
'Do you think you've recovered?' I ask. 'I think I've a head injury,'
she replies.

Yes, little things just haven't tied up. She said she knew my road –
Balmoral – from years as a trade unionist, but then phoned several
times on the way. She pronounced 'rapport' *report* early in the
evening, and later correctly.

Sometimes I find people with a learning challenge have a lovely
immediate way of being in the world.

simply

Living a life of
simplicity is perhaps
the greatest gift
we can give
ourselves.

my writing

Don't
want to be
smart.

Just
to be me.
To have
tears in
my eyes.

I like writing. Raw writing. I must have regular raw hot-off-life writing. 'Cause then I see what matters. And that's everything. The temperature of the heater, the bug on the wood, my itchy bottom, each and every feeling, each and every cloud. Anything excluded? Nope. Don't think so.

words

Words.

Say what you mean.

Right speech.

Buddhists talk about *right speech*. I like that. It's about saying what you need to say. It makes life simpler.

need

Wondering
how it would be
to live from
my place
of need.

I'd be packing up – slowly – to live closer to Elizabeth (H).

my largest organ

My skin
is the whole of me.
Porous, can breathe.
Holds me, hides me.
Knows my pain, irritation.

Kindly touch.

plaits

A plait is such a beautiful thing.

Is there anything else like it?

For how many of us is our childhood memory tied up with plaits?

Mom yanked my scalp – it was painful – as she plaited my hair
tightly. My father had this daft (Baptist) idea that her hair is a
woman's glory and so our hair was long. (There were various
ribbons – navy for school. They're a rare commodity now.)
Till we got lice and had it all cut off.

When I did my thanksgiving ceremony I bound three rich cords
in a plait as part of the centre-piece to represent the three languages
I know and love – Afrikaans, English, isiXhosa. Two other cords
were twisted representing my two main faith traditions –
Christianity and Buddhism.

in praise of play

Whales spend
three times as much time playing
as they do
searching for
food.[7]

I love
that.

In our Karuna training Maura Sills said: 'Never more than
25% effort!'[8]

7. Jungle Theatre's play about whales (Cape Town).
8. Core Process Psychotherapy training at the Karuna Institute, Devon, England.

diy

Always said
I found
women who can
wield a drill
sexy.

I am awed by women who can strip and re-do a whole house –
as Claudie did.

And today I'm trying to paint just above the skirting board in my
practice room. The maintenance man said I wouldn't need to use
masking tape. I immediately make a mess and try to clean it and
then cover the skirting board with tape. I make the mess worse.
The tape won't come off the roll properly. When did I last use a
roller? The rolling part has come off. I try and fit it on again. I get
full of paint. I can't get it back on properly and now it can hardly
fit into the tin. And I still got paint on the skirting board 'cause
I didn't think I needed to cover it completely.

Persevering – in most things – seems the name of the game.
I suspect we often give up just before we get there. (As an
acquaintance put it last night: 'god answers prayers at the very
last moment!').

depression

I'm
curious
about depression.

I'm starting to notice that the things that are most important to us we never speak about – like childbirth and depression. I've started to ask people who I know have had experience of depression how they would describe it. One said: 'It's all pervasive – it affects everything'. Another: 'It's like carrying around a heavy backpack – and you can't put it down'.

I think the word might be wrong. What if we called it sadness, melancholy?

One in four of us will suffer from this.

It must surely be telling us something about our lives, how we live. Maybe saying: hey wait, something's wrong here and needs attention.

We don't connect with each other very well so people who are having a hard time can be very alone in this.

Doctors who prescribe medication I'm sure are trying to help. You feel helpless in the face of another's sadness.

Mark Rice-Oxley who has written of his own experience says four things helped him: 'Meditation, love, time and therapy.'[9]

Can we talk more about this? There's wisdom in it. We're in this together.

9. 'Depression: The illness that is still taboo' in *Mail & Guardian* August 6-12 2010 p 17-19.

walking

Am
doing a lot of
walking around and
catching trains.

Mostly we're happy
doing ordinary things.

During the 2010 soccer World Cup in Cape Town the highlight for
so many was walking the fan walk – a stretch of about two kilometres
from the station to the stadium. Sure, there was entertainment along
the way, but the main thing was people got a real kick out of walking
together with people from all over the world, but more particularly I
think with people from their own country who they never 'walk with'.
People got so happy! Many middle-class people took the train – they
may never have done this before or not for years – and they loved it.

sure-ness

It seems
when I'm most sure
about something
that I'm the most
wrong.

I quite like the contrari-ness of this.

family

society

living

loving

coma

I was
always a bit scared
of patients
in a coma.

I did a period of voluntary work at a hospice. I would go with my
guitar and sit quietly at people's bedsides, maybe singing a bit –
songs that the person would know, in their language.

I can remember the older woman lying there, her mouth slightly
open. I didn't stay long with her. I feel sorry now.

Comacare started in Cape Town. Jan, the founder, says: 'Don't wish
the person out of a coma. It's a healing time.'

Apparently you can have a full relationship with a comatose person.
The person may give sounds or do movements that you can respond
to. You can communicate in a very rich way.

known

Sawubona –
We are seeing you.

A greeting in isiZulu[10].

"It has been said that 'A person is enlightened when someone looks at them'. A person is enlightened when another loves them."[11]

10. One of the many South African languages.
11. *The Impact of God: Soundings from St John of the Cross*, Iain Matthew 1995 London: Hodder and Stoughton, p 28.

I'd like that

Move
closer and closer apart[12].

I like the phrase.

I'd like to be with you in that way.

('Let's be alone together, let's see if we're that strong' is how
Leonard Cohen puts it[13].)

12. John Bayley speaking of his relationship with Iris Murdoch in *Iris: A memoir of Iris Murdoch* 1998 London: Gerald Duckworth & Co.Ltd., p 39.
13. In *Waiting for The Miracle* produced by Leonard Cohen and Yoav Goren 1992 Sony Music Entertainment.

not going away

It was
quite easy really –
learning to
stay.

He'd turned his face to the wall – in every way. When I visited –
in the care home – he wouldn't connect with me.

They'd put him there. The twins lived in London. Having Frank at
home in the rambling house on his zimmer frame was unsafe and
didn't suit them. He may fall and they'd have to leave their lives –
and her house in Spain – and attend.

And me, the sort of carer, living in the flat above him, really seeing
if he was alive every day … and soon coming to love him.

And they insisted. And he tried. The first week or two being assisted
by well presented women was a novelty. But then, no. He made his
no known. Late, too late, the doctor said: 'He's pining'. By then all
the taking to his bed, face to the wall, had caused fluid to go to his
lungs. They came the Friday. Too late, the thought to move him
home. To hospital, and there to die about five days later.

But you'd said: 'Stay, don't go', when he wouldn't look at me on
my visits. And so I stayed. And I learnt to love to stay. And in the
hospital bed I touched his skin, stroked his fore-head. I stayed and
stayed and stayed.

Thank you Elizabeth.

at rest

On the train
I most
see / feel
the child –
suckling or
resting on the mother's breast.

I see the way women handle their babies in the train. Men too.
It touches me. The child is everything. Others sitting alongside
admire the child. There is such reverence, tenderness.

Often the woman has the child on her back, then the child rests on
her belly as she sits down.

I remember on my first quiet day / retreat we were asked our image
of God. Mine was something like that – being in the lap of an
African woman.

Elizabeth November 2012

I would
like
to be able
to *rest* in you a little
more.

I'd like to be the one
you come home to.

emptiness

theory

There's
something about
theory
that's
bothering me
at present.

Surely any theory needs to be very close to experience. It's a
delicate thing. One's experience can feel so subtle, so fragile.
To have a theory thrust upon it can feel gross, unkind.

I would agree with Thich Nhat Hanh[14] that knowledge can be an
obstacle to our understanding.

Buddhism and psychology – both disciplines dedicated to
understanding the human condition and alleviating suffering –
often feel very theory-full. I like what Meister Eckhart says –
god is known by subtraction rather than addition.

14. *Being Peace* 1987 Berkeley: Parallax Press, p 42.

ignorance

I prefer the
word

'ignorance'

to 'sin'.

Christians speak of sin. Buddhists more of ignorance – sometimes
of confusion. This feels more forgiving. Jesus spoke like that:
'Please forgive them, they don't know what they're doing'.

a psalm

I need
to write a psalm.

Psalms were ways writers expressed themselves; a lament –
how long will you forget me my Beloved? – or praise –
everything you do is so good.

What will *I* express?

Psalm 1

Beloved.

May I think of you in the morning? Does that intrude?

May I think of you at midday too?

You live in Birmingham, I in Cape Town.

May I think of you at evening?

Psalm 2

The morning
feels an important time.

We don't any more say
prayers then, nor at night.

What then might frame our days?

mates

'There's something else,'… she said, clearly emotional.
It was close to the end of our time together, so I said:
'You don't have to tell me today unless you want to'.
I was anticipating she was going to tell me about some
difficulty. 'No, it's something good,' she said. 'It was
Christ and the Buddha. They were both holding me –
holding me very close'. Our eyes filled with tears.

Perhaps we should never separate them.

the prayer-stool

There
doesn't seem to
want to be
a separate thing
called 'prayer'.

In my study (where I used to see clients before I turned the garage into a practice room) I have my computer, two lounge chairs, an old tattered red mat and a prayer stool. Sometimes I place the stool on the mat and light a candle to do a thing I think will be 'prayer'. No, it can't happen – at least not at present. It seems to suggest going to another place, a sort of re-booting myself in a certain way

So for now I think I better give up. Though I'll leave the stool where it is.

it's down

Why
do people persist in
thinking faith /
spiritual practice is about
going *up*?

Of course it's not.
It's about
going

      d

      o

      w

      n.

I'm cross that we've been so confused. Is this why we've stuffed
up the planet – as everything is about going *up*, ascending from
the earth?

Religious leaders speak of all paths ascending the mountain.
All paths reach the summit, they say.

No. You're wrong.

It's like this. You go down, down, down. Deep into the body
of the earth. And there each tradition joins one deep subterranean
stream. We join *down*, not up.

silence – night

At seven (in the morning)
it's dark
in the street
as I leave.

Something
beautiful.

Like silence.

I would like to be more a person of the night.

Perhaps I live my night by day?

Silence is
space –
part of my body structure,
cells.

What pace is silence?

dark matter

Mostly
we just don't know.

I love that.

Most of our universe comprises dark matter[15] of which we know
very little. The stars and planets that astronomers see make up only
about 4% of the universe.

Buddhists call it 'empty mind'. Mostly, we think we know far
too much.

15. I think this is a fairly new term – I've been reading of it the last few years.

god loves you

It was a Skype link up with Dakar. The South African government had refused the Dalai Lama a visa to attend Tutu's 80th birthday celebrations. (Desmond was in Cape Town, South Africa.)

Desmond
spoke of civil liberties,
the Dalai Lama of
the love of god.

(I think he said:
'god loves you'.)

I love it when you can't guess – or you'd guess wrong – which faith tradition people are from. I love it when the Buddhists speak more about god than the Christians.

to bed

How
I go to bed
matters.

It matters how I go to bed.

I wonder about evenings. I guess in earlier times this would be
the part of the day when we'd gather together in the firelight.

I'd like to find my modern equivalent.

wondering

What

if I lived

at the speed

of my body?

I love atheism, secularism, (parts of) Christianity, Buddhism.
And some of Islam that I've been exposed to.

And what compass do *I* choose by which to live?

I want to inhabit my body. To live in time, in tune with *my* form.
This often means slowing down. Pausing maybe, stopping.
Sensing into even just the body's pulse. Being at rest in my flesh
and blood.

Is this not praise and thanks?

silence – words – silence

The
silence from which
words come.

The words from which
silence comes.

The title of the writing course – *the silence from which words come* –
caught my attention and I enrolled. I found myself, in the class,
doing a piece that also spoke of *the words from which silence comes.*

I want that for the reader.

And pleasure-in-relating.

Thanks to

First readers: Elizabeth, Lindsay, Sean – for your necessary encouragement at that stage.

Toni Stuart – for The Silence from which Words Come – for helping it happen.

Nelisa Ngqulana - writing partner at a critical time.

Colleen Higgs – for pleasant collaboration.

Na'eemah Masoet – for warmth, professionalism and great editing.

To those who said they were honoured to appear in the collection – by name or otherwise.

Jacobus November – *Big Issue* vendor and part of their art project – for stunning cover image.

All our ancestors. May we all be at rest.

Other Hands-On poetry titles:

A Lioness At My Heels – Robin Winckel-Mellish
Difficult to Explain –Finuala Dowling
Lava Lamp Poems – Colleen Higgs
Absent Tongues – Kelwyn Sole